100

THINGS TO DO IN
SEATTLE
BEFORE YOU
DIE

2nd Edition

100
THINGS TO DO IN
SEATTLE
BEFORE YOU
DIE

JACOB UITTI

REEDY PRESS

Library of Congress Control Number: 2018936118

ISBN: 9781681061474

Design by Jill Halpin
All photos by Morgen Schuler

Printed in the United States of America
18 19 20 21 22   5 4 3 2 1

Please note that websites, phone numbers, addresses, and company names are subject to change or cancellation. We did our best to relay the most accurate information available, but due to circumstances beyond our control, please do not hold us liable for misinformation. When exploring new destinations, please do your homework before you go.

DEDICATION

This book is dedicated to anyone who arrives in Seattle like I did some ten years ago, with a few suitcases full of clothes and a bunch of curiosity, in search of a wondrous city. This book is also dedicated to my mom because I love her.

• •

CONTENTS

Music and Entertainment

• •

Sports and Recreation

Culture and History

• •

Shopping And Fashion

ACKNOWLEDGMENTS

I'd like to thank all the generous spirits in this great city who have shown me their favorite restaurants, performance halls, tap houses, and anything and everything else that has kept me afloat spiritually and culturally. Seattle is rich with people who care.

INTRODUCTION

Seattle has been my home now for more than ten years. I moved here at age twenty-four from New Jersey and the city has expanded and blossomed before my eyes in thoughtful, majestic, and head-scratching ways ever since. Along with everyone else in the city, I've seen it change and evolve over the last decade. With the influx of tech workers, artists, and those interested in the beautiful outdoors that the Emerald City and the greater Pacific Northwest offer, Seattle is a prime destination for anyone who likes innovation, culture, and nature. It's a hub for independent music, tech, food, and craft beer. In other words, it's a paradise with much to do—from chomping on a basket of fried crickets at a Seattle Mariners baseball game to quaffing a craft cocktail during a burlesque performance beneath historic Pike Place Market. And this book is my little bit of reverence for all that's possible in the city. Enjoy, and thank you for reading.

FOOD AND DRINK

EAT AFTER HOURS
AT BETH'S CAFÉ

If, when you check your watch, the hour is much later than you'd thought and your stomach is grumbling, then you need to stop by Beth's Café for a bite to eat. Almost anyone who's stayed in Seattle long enough to call it home has passed through Beth's simple dining room. The decades-old diner serves breakfast twenty-four hours a day—giant, twelve-egg omelets; pizza pan-sized pancakes piled high with strawberries and whipped cream; and so many strips of bacon that they would, if lined up, likely wrap around the earth multiple times over. But don't be surprised if you see someone wobbling a bit betwixt the crayon-colored menus hanging on the walls from the whiskey he had earlier at some other establishment. Everyone gets hungry and, as such, everyone loves Beth's.

7311 Aurora Ave. N., 206-782-5588
bethscafe.com

A *TWIN PEAKS*-INSPIRED GETAWAY

Set in the pastoral expanse of Washington State, David Lynch's acclaimed television show, *Twin Peaks,* recently revived, has grown well beyond a local favorite. It is beloved by viewers all over the world, many of whom might even wish they could jump from their sofas into the television sets. Well, if you're in Seattle, Snoqualmie Falls, where some of the show was filmed, is close by. Visually stunning, the area has become famous throughout the world for the backdrop it provided the show. Thousands flock here yearly to get a slice of cherry pie and a cup of coffee from Twede's Café, where so many indelible scenes were shot. And, if you plan ahead, you may even be able to get a table at the picturesque Salish Lodge, the face of the eerie television show's theme song, which overlooks the beautiful signature waterfall.

Twede's Café
137 W. North Bend Way, North Bend, 425-831-5511
twedescafe.com

Salish Lodge
6501 Railroad Ave. SE, Snoqualmie, 425-888-2556
salishlodge.com

SNACK EVERYWHERE
IN PIKE PLACE MARKET

On the street level, there's the obvious: fishmongers tossing trout and salmon to one another to wrap for sale while an audience gathers. Just a few booths down, if you have a sweet tooth, you can sample a strand of chocolate spaghetti from a noodle vendor. Pike Place Market, which is one of the oldest farmers markets in the United States, contains so much variety that it's the perfect place for the peckish or the positively starving. Visit the catacombs beneath for excellent dumplings, or try out one of the surrounding restaurants for cured meats or gnocchi. The market, which opened in 1907, is the supreme destination for the hungry traveler, offering everything from artisan bread samples to bites of the freshest cheese curds on earth.

First Ave. and Pike St., 206-682-7453
pikeplacemarket.org

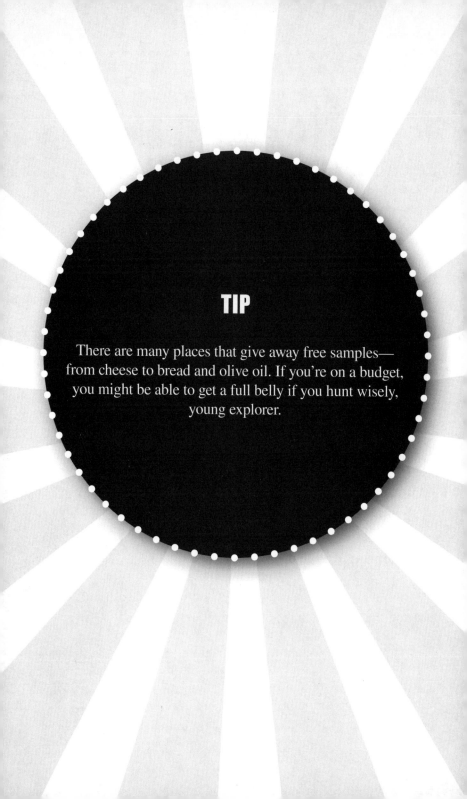

TIP

There are many places that give away free samples—from cheese to bread and olive oil. If you're on a budget, you might be able to get a full belly if you hunt wisely, young explorer.

RELAX WITH AN OLD-FASHIONED
AT ZIG ZAG CAFÉ

Your thumb and index finger hold your glass just so. It's quiet in the cocktail lounge but for the clinking of a few glasses. Suddenly, from a table in the corner, comes a burst of laughter, and the otherwise still air mixes with mirth for a pleasant break from the real world. Sometimes you really can steal a few minutes alone, satisfied. And Zig Zag, perhaps Seattle's most renowned cocktail lounge, is a perfect place to do just that. Inside, you're transported to a timeless place where spirits are the sole focus. Enjoy classic drinks, or delve into newer, innovative cocktails like the Staggerly, made with rye, aquavit, and Nardini Amaro, or the Pierre, with bourbon, apricot liqueur, and lemon juice, as your moment of repose slides into a full night of enjoyment.

1501 Western Ave., Ste. 202, 206-625-1146
zigzagseattle.com

TAKE IN THE CITY
FROM THE SPACE NEEDLE

As you're seated, look through the expansive windows and see the entire city below. Catch a glimpse of the gangly statue standing in Gas Works Park—only much smaller than you're used to. The rotating restaurant atop the Seattle Space Needle offers a 360-degree view of the picturesque city. Share an appetizer while Lake Washington passes by below. See the glass statues reflecting the sunlight in the Chihuly Garden while your waiter brings you dessert. Built for the 1962 Century 21 Exposition, a world's fair, the most famous monument in Seattle has had some of the city's most well-known musicians (read: Pearl Jam's Mike McCready) perform from the top deck, more than six hundred feet above ground. It's also the home of the city's annual fireworks displays and a perfect place to watch the city pass by while sharing a bottle of wine.

400 Broad St., 1-800-937-9582
spaceneedle.com

TIP
The Space Needle is currently undergoing renovation and, at press, does not have a reopen date. Check with the Space Needle before visiting.

MAKE MAGIC HAPPEN
WITH YOU AND THEO
CHOCOLATE FACTORY

Sitting in the lounge of the Theo Chocolate factory, waiting for the tour to begin, you're given plastic-baggie things to put on your shoes and the top of your head. It's a precaution that ensures their moneymaker confections stay pure and unsullied while you watch how they're made. Seattle's version of Willy Wonka's famed factory, Theo Chocolate educates its consumer before offering its delicious creations, including salted almond butter cups, ghost chili caramels, raspberry chocolate bars, and peppermint chocolate clusters. Every tour at the factory begins with a tutorial about sourcing sustainable cocoa beans and ends in the glorious, candy-filled gift shop. Feel like a kid in a candy store no matter your age as you sift through delicious options right after walking through the factory catacombs filled with giant ovens.

3400 Phinney Ave. N., 206-632-5100
theochocolate.com/factory-tours

POP A BOTTLE
AT CHATEAU STE. MICHELLE

It's best to bring a blanket and pack a picnic if you're venturing to the rolling landscape that is the Chateau Ste. Michelle Winery. Located in nearby Woodinville, the destination, which opened more than fifty years ago, creates some of the most popular bottled beverages in the Northwest, including a highly rated cabernet sauvignon and late-harvest Riesling. The facility also offers on-site tours, tastings, and chef-created wine-paired dinners. But the pièce de résistance might be the annual summer concert series, which has showcased musical luminaries like Allen Stone, Rodrigo y Gabriela, Elvis Costello, John Legend, and ZZ Top. Music and wine might just end up being the ultimate pairing, especially while the Northwest sun sets overhead and songs are heard from grass to grove.

14111 NE 145th St., Woodinville, 425-488-1133
ste-michelle.com

LATTE
LIKE A LOCAL

If you gathered ten people and asked them to close their eyes and say the first thing that came to mind when you said "Seattle," a great many would immediately say "coffee." Starbucks was born here, after all. And you can still visit the original location in Pike Place Market to grab a latte and see where it all began. But if you want to stray from the touristy side of the espresso cup and hit some authentic neighborhood spots, we recommend visiting Espresso Vivace, a classic boutique shop where many on the north side of town grab their joe. Or, in the South End, the bustling neighborhood community hub The Station, famous for its annual block party summer music showcase, is a crowd favorite (hint: try the spicy Mexican Latte).

Original Starbucks at Pike Place Market
1912 Pike Pl., 206-448-8762
starbucks.com

Espresso Vivace (Brix location)
532 Broadway Ave. E., 206-860-2722
espressovivace.com/retail/brix

The Station
1600 S. Roberto Maestas Festival St., 206-453-4892
thestationbh.com

SAVOR
OPRAH'S FAVORITE FRIED CHICKEN

Oprah doesn't mess around. When the queen of tastemakers knows what she likes, she sticks to it and tells the world. So when she tried Ezell Stephens's fried chicken in Seattle one gray day, she knew she had to fly him out to cook it for her birthday that same year—and that's exactly what she did. Stephens is the king of fried chicken in Seattle. A veteran of the Coast Guard, he moved to Seattle a few decades ago and opened up his shop, which soon grew in popularity and then became famous thanks to Oprah. Stephens's first restaurant was simply called Ezell's Famous Chicken. But he's since departed from that chain. Now, Stephens owns and operates Heaven Sent Fried Chicken, and it's the city's landmark location to get some of the best breaded bird, mac 'n' cheese, and biscuits in the area.

Ezell's Famous Chicken
501 Twenty-Third Ave., 206-324-4141
ezellschicken.com

Heaven Sent Fried Chicken
509 S. Third St., Renton, 425-917-3000
heavensentfriedchicken.com

TIP
At Heaven Sent, order the spicy chicken strips.
They're some of the best you'll ever taste.

EAT A PIZZA
BIGGER THAN YOUR FRONT SEAT

There are a surprisingly large number of excellent pizza places to try in Seattle. While New York and Chicago are better known for their pies, Seattle is no slouch. The Emerald City is home to excellent deep-dish, wood-fired, Neapolitan, and East Coast styles of the good, cheesy stuff. But if you're going to try just one option, make it Italian Family Pizza, which serves pizza pies so gigantic that the box may not fit in your car to take home. You'll at least have to adjust the seats to get it in the back. With a simple red-checkered-tablecloth aesthetic, the restaurant brings traditional pizzeria style to the Northwest. And while their pizzas can be topped with pepperoni, meatballs, basil, extra cheese, or any number of other options, nothing tops Italian Family Pizza for a slice.

1028 Madison St., 206-538-0040
italianfamilypizza.juisyfood.com

TRY
THE COUNTRY'S BEST IPA

If there's one thing you can count on in Seattle, it's a wealth of microbreweries. It seems like every week a new one pops up in Ballard or Fremont or Greenwood. But one of the city's best and most recognizable options is definitely Georgetown Brewing Company, located in the city's South End industrial neighborhood. Winner of two gold medals in 2016 at the Great American Beer Festival, the brewery's Bodhizafa IPA was voted tops for Best American India Pale Ale, victorious among more than three hundred national entries. Brewery cofounder Manny Chao is also the namesake for the city's favorite pale ale, Manny's, the perfect entry-level beer for any hopeful hophead. And Georgetown Brewing offers a cozy taproom where thirsty visitors can try new concoctions fresh from the kettles.

5200 Denver Ave. S., 206-766-8055
georgetownbeer.com

TIP
Georgetown often offers tours of its facility. There's something special about seeing the inner workings from whence your beer came that adds to the sipping experience, so try and get a behind-the-scenes look.

WIN THE NIGHT
AT SHORTY'S

There's a specific thrill that occurs when you play an arcade game. It starts with a jolt in your chest and bursts out through your fingertips as you control the character on screen or slap at a silver pinball. And, as an adult, you can pair this exhilaration with pints of beer and stiff mixed drinks. In Seattle, there may be no better place to do that than at Shorty's, located in Seattle's historic Pioneer Square neighborhood. The bar, equipped with a robust Coney Island-inspired hot dog menu, is packed wall to wall with pinball games, both rare and recognizable. The bar, which has been around for decades, has only increased in popularity over the last handful of years. In fact, if you ask Shorty's proprietor, he'll tell you that the game bar is responsible for today's modern pinball resurgence.

2222 Second Ave., 206-441-5449
shortydog.com

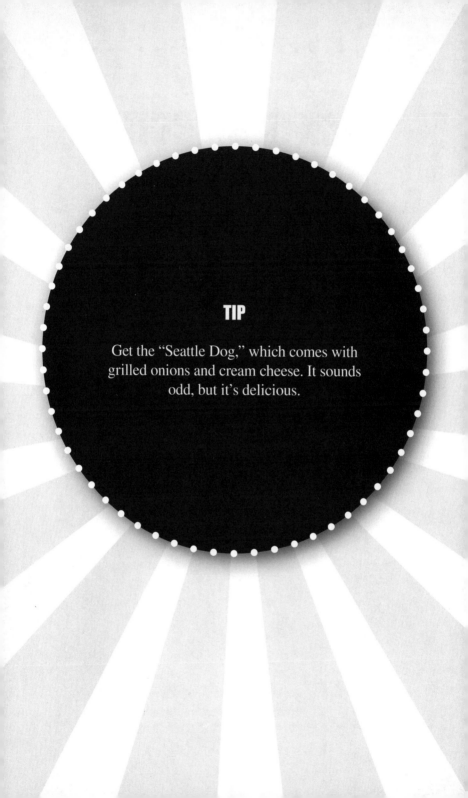

TIP

Get the "Seattle Dog," which comes with grilled onions and cream cheese. It sounds odd, but it's delicious.

BASK IN BISCUITS
FOR BREAKFAST

Opening your eyes after a late night out, one of the first things that pops to mind is breakfast. While omelets, pancakes, and waffles are the obvious choice, the Emerald City has a batch of terrific biscuit places to make your breakfast or brunch experience top-notch. Before any other, you must try the Southern-style eatery The Wandering Goose, which serves perhaps the most satisfying plate of food in Seattle: a fried chicken biscuit sandwich doused in delicious sausage gravy. While the restaurant offers supremely tasty food, it can often be packed. If you find yourself in a long line, check out Morsel, in the bustling University District, which is also popular for offering premium biscuit sandwiches, made tangy and delicious with their house-made signature tomato jam.

The Wandering Goose
403 Fifteenth Ave. E., 206-323-9938
thewanderinggoose.com

Morsel
4754 University Way NE, 206-268-0154
morselseattle.com

GET THE SCOOP
AT MOLLY MOON'S

It's been said that Seattle consumes the most ice cream per capita of any city in the entire United States. Whether or not that's true, what is clear is that Seattleites don't mind standing in line rain or shine to get their favorite sundaes or cones. While there are many independent craft ice cream shops—some known for being inventive, others known for pairing ice cream with arcade games and comics—the city's standout shop has to be Molly Moon's. The establishment, which boasts several locations throughout the city, is famous for its clean but creative flavors like its renowned strawberry balsamic, which pairs perfectly with a scoop of chocolate or vanilla bean, topped with hot fudge.

1/2 1622 N. Forty-Fifth St., 206-547-5105
mollymoon.com

SLURP UP SEATTLE NOODLES
ALL OVER THE CITY

I need to confess something: noodles are my favorite food. And living in Seattle means there are many, many delicious noodle options. So, for your dining pleasure, here is a quick crash course on the city's best noodle houses. For Italian-style pasta, try the melt-in-your-mouth Tajarin noodles with butter and sage from Cascina Spinasse. For a bowl of artisan, aromatic pho, visit Ba Bar. For the city's best street food, pork ramen, check out Ooink. For specialty western Chinese hand-shaven wide noodles in hot oil sauce, visit Xi'an Noodles. For world-famous soup dumplings, check out Din Tai Fung. And for dim sum, Joy Palace. Whew, that's a mouthful!

Cascina Spinasse
1531 Fourteenth Ave., 206-251-7673
spinasse.com

Ba Bar
550 Twelfth Ave., 206-328-2030
babarseattle.com

Ooink
1416 Harvard Ave., 206-568-7669
ooinkwa.com

Xi'an Noodles
5259 University Way NE, 206-522-8888
facebook.com/XIANNOODLES/

Din Tai Fung (University Village)
2621 NE Forty-Sixth St., 206-525-0958
dintaifungusa.com

Joy Palace
6030 Martin Luther King Jr. Way S., 206-723-4066
joypalaceseattle.com

DEVOUR PASTRIES
IN WEST SEATTLE

When you walk in, the glass case looks like a giant treasure trove. It brims with croissants, *pain au chocolat,* breads, cookies of all sorts, and other delicious treats that, when gazing at them, make you remember being a child, tugging on your mother's coat, hoping for something special to eat. But now you hold the purse strings. It's time for whatever your heart desires in the little bakery nestled off the city's beaten path in West Seattle. Bakery Nouveau was once a well-kept secret, but now it is most certainly a known quantity among its droves of customers. It may be hard to choose between the croissant sandwiches or berry-topped Danishes, but that's why the world created more than one meal.

4737 California Ave. SW, 206-923-0534
bakerynouveau.com

BUY THE FARM
IN BALLARD

We all have moments in which we realize that life is truly wonderful. For some, it's that first ride down the driveway with a new bike. For others, it's reaching out and grabbing the first bouquet of giant purple carrots from the Ballard Farmers Market. Washington is rich with local farmers, which means Seattle is rich with local farmers markets—with popular options popping up in Columbia City, Capitol Hill, and Fremont. But the year-round collection of Washington farmers who take over multiple blocks in Ballard is the city's prize. Featuring delicious hot food stands, mini doughnuts, and more bushels of fresh flowers, fruit, meats, and vegetables than you can imagine, the Ballard Farmers Market on Sundays is well worth traversing the teams of eager organic shoppers to get to your favorite snack and groceries for the week.

Twenty-Second Ave. NW & NW Market St.
sfmamarkets.com

REVEL IN A FOOD CARNIVAL
AT UWAJIMAYA

When you notice the bag of Green Tea KitKat bars, you realize you're not in Kansas anymore. With an unassuming exterior and a flabbergasting and huge interior, Uwajimaya is one of the most exciting places to visit if you have a hankering for a fun—and possibly new—food option. With aisles of imported chili sauces, soft drinks, exotic candies, locally sourced seafood, noodles (dried and fresh), and many other options not available in more traditional American grocery stores, Uwajimaya offers an array of delicacies for hungry shoppers. Seaweed chips? Yes. Cookies and cream Pocky sticks? Yup. Blueberry mochi? Indeed! It's the perfect place to meander for an hour to find new dinner ideas or to get those hard-to-find ingredients you always seem to crave.

600 Fifth Ave. S., 206-624-6248
uwajimaya.com

FALL IN LOVE
WITH ALL THAT WOW

When you walk through the doors of the Triple XXX Root Beer Drive-in, about fifteen minutes outside of Seattle in Issaquah, owner Jose Enciso wants you to say "Wow!" over and over again. And, really, there's no way you won't. The 1950s-style diner, which hosts a classic car show almost every weekend, offers giant, messy burgers and giant, messy milkshakes accompanied by giant, messy plates of fries and onion rings that satisfy like the first time you had them when you were young. With model Cadillac cars hanging from the ceilings like a child's mobile and stickers slapped on nearly every inch of wall space, the restaurant is practically a landmark for wonderment and a reminder of a classic era, displayed through the lens of Enciso's friendly, charming, and boisterous demeanor.

98 NE Gilman Blvd., Issaquah, 425-392-1266
triplexrootbeer.com

TIP
This one is simple. No matter what, get a milkshake. They're the best in the region, both to look at and to drink.

POKE
IN THE DELI

Leave it to Seattleites to create a popular new raw fish eatery in the back of a corner store. In this era of do-it-yourself sharing culture, Seattle often leads the way when it comes to culinary innovation, so why not try out one of the city's hottest dishes in a Stop N Shop deli? The concept of poke, a Hawaiian dish consisting of marinated raw fish served over rice with vegetables, has spread like wildfire in the Emerald City. Because it's a dish that doesn't require much besides a fridge and prep space, poke is often served in bars that can pop up anywhere. One the city's most popular happens to be in a little corner store in the Wallingford neighborhood. So poke your head in and sample one of the city's hottest new crazes served chilled—like eel, snapper, or salmon—as a salad, as part of a burrito, or in a bowl.

2323 N. Forty-Fifth St., 206-708-1882
facebook.com/45th-Stop-N-Shop-Poke-Bar-1711806935698312/

OTHER PLACES TO TRY

Dick's Drive-In for a great hamburger, Westward for seafood and an amazing lakeside view, Tacos Chukis for excellent pork tacos, and Yoroshiku for more amazing ramen.

Dick's Drive-In
111 NE Forty-Fifth St., 206-632-5125
ddir.com

Westward
2501 N. Northlake Way, 206-552-8215
westwardseattle.com

Tacos Chukis
219 Broadway E., 206-328-4447
facebook.com/TacosChukis

Yoroshiku
1911 N. Forty-Fifth St., 206-547-4649
yoroshikuseattle.com

MUSIC AND ENTERTAINMENT

HAVE A CUP
OF COFFEE AT KEXP

If music is the lifeblood of Seattle, KEXP 90.3 FM is the pumping heart. The station, which is the largest non-NPR public radio broadcaster in the country, plays commercial-free local, independent, and international music twenty-four hours a day, every day. The DJs are local celebrities, and the live in-studio performances the station books, records, and releases on video have been streamed tens of millions of times over. For something so vital, you might think the building would be protected by a twenty-foot moat. But, no, you're free to walk into the KEXP headquarters, head to La Marzocco, the little coffee shop inside, order a latte, and watch it all happen through the DJ glass. And who knows? You may even see Beck or Chris Ballew from The Presidents of the United States of America walk in with their latest release for the airwaves.

KEXP 90.3 FM and La Marzocco Café
472 First Ave. N.
kexp.org

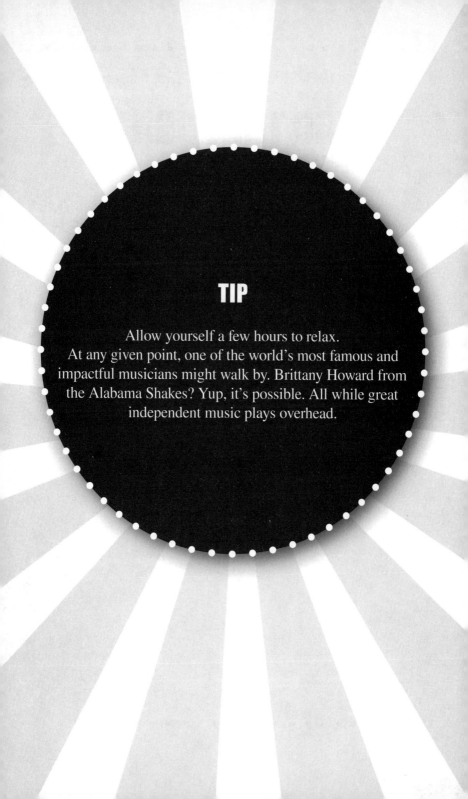

TIP

Allow yourself a few hours to relax.
At any given point, one of the world's most famous and impactful musicians might walk by. Brittany Howard from the Alabama Shakes? Yup, it's possible. All while great independent music plays overhead.

DIG THROUGH
EMERALD CITY CRATES

You know a city is serious about its vinyl when there's a record shop in the airport. And at the Seattle-Tacoma International Airport, you can stop by the Sub Pop Record Shop pre- or post-flight and purchase an album by any of the iconic label's artists—from Nirvana to Father John Misty. In the city itself, however, record collectors should make sure to swing by Easy Street in West Seattle, where you can get the clearest sense of the local music scene—local artists have consigned their albums there for thirty years, from Macklemore to Pearl Jam to Sir Mix-a-Lot—combined with an extensive collection of artists from all over the globe. And what's especially great about Easy Street is that it boasts its own café with music-inspired breakfast dishes, coffee, and craft beer on hand.

Sub Pop Records (Airport)
17801 International Blvd., SeaTac, 206-441-8441
subpop.com

Easy Street Records
4559 California Ave. SW, 206-938-3279
easystreetonline.com

GO SQUARE DANCIN'
AT THE LITTLE RED HEN

In the Netflix series *Master of None,* the main characters wonder the meaning of the term "honky-tonk." They eventually travel to Nashville and find out. Seems reasonable. But they could have just as easily flown to Seattle to see what's what because at the Little Red Hen, where the floors are pre-sawdusted and the whiskey bottles are pre-stocked, dancers can sign up for boot-jangling authentic free square dance lessons Sunday through Tuesday nights. Then, those same nights, or on a more rousing weekend evening, you can perfect your moves as the famed ten-piece local band Country Lips plays fiddle- and banjo-laden songs into the Pacific Western night. Hook an elbow and shake a tail feather—it's a welcome bit of the Old West in the city that birthed grunge.

7115 Woodlawn Ave. NE, 206-522-1168
littleredhen.com

TIP
Spring for top-shelf whiskey. Your body will thank you in the morning.

SING YOUR HEART OUT
AT RICKSHAW

Few combinations ensure a fun and lively night better than karaoke in a dive bar. But when you add those to a menu teaming with delicious food options—like steaming plates of General Tso's chicken, fried rice, and egg rolls—you are assured memorable and friendly fulfillment. At Rickshaw Restaurant & Lounge, boisterous karaoke plays seven nights a week, bringing in droves of regulars ready to cavort shoulder to shoulder to the sounds of some good ol' Billy Joel or The Notorious B.I.G. Blaring through speakers in the tight, nostalgic quarters, novices and experts alike share their favorite tunes before taking a box of noodles to go. Euphoric gin-and-tonic drinkers sway together while they follow the lyrics their buddies— say, a bachelorette, a Navy man, or a neighborhood regular—belt out the songs they were always meant to perform.

322 N. 105th St., 206-789-0120
therickshaw.net

PAY HOMAGE
TO THE WORLD'S GREATEST GUITARIST

On the south end of Broadway, right in front of giant art supplies store Blick Art Materials, stands a beautiful bronze statue of the late, great Jimi Hendrix, the world's greatest rock guitar player. Hendrix, who was born in Seattle on November 27, 1942, grew up in the city and learned how to play on a five-dollar acoustic. While he went on to international success, he remained tied to Seattle, and many of his family members live here to this day. The statue, created in homage to the guitar god by developer Mike Malone, shows the musician wailing, guitar turned upside down in signature fashion, his face absorbed and entranced, as if receiving the music from the heavens. Complete with bell-bottoms and a headband, the statue evokes all the best about the music icon.

1600 Broadway, 206-324-0750
dickblick.com/stores/washington/seattle

CATCH A CONCERT
AT KEY

On a recent December night, the locally grown and platinum-selling hip-hop artist Macklemore, strung up by wires from the ceiling of KeyArena, mic in hand, was rapping, as the crowd cheered like mad. That same night, arena officials raised a banner in the rapper's honor for selling out five straight shows in the 17,500-person venue. The emcee, humbled, bowed and thanked his fans. At the historic KeyArena, audiences are privy to giant, memorable shows like this on what seems like a regular basis—from Lorde to Jay-Z to Pink—all in the confines of one of the country's coziest arenas. Located smack-dab in the middle of the bustling Seattle Center complex, which hosts regular food and beverage tastings and local music festivals, KeyArena is the booming embodiment of Seattle's love for music.

305 Harrison St., 206-684-7200
keyarena.com

EXPERIENCE JAZZ
THROUGH A COCKTAIL STRAW

Slip into the 1920s at Vito's Lounge. Standing unassumingly in Seattle's First Hill neighborhood, like a gentleman with his hat low under a lamppost, Vito's is classic. Inside, it's a robust mixture of some of the city's best jazz musicians and cocktails made both delicate and strong. Local luminaries all play sets here, from members of platinum-selling bands to those who soon will be, and Vito's attracts aficionados of the art along with those who have a taste for a good meal and a good drink. It's not required, but you might want to dress your best and snuggle up with your date in a dark corner booth while the upright bassist begins his bowed solo. Order the charred Caesar salad and a martini, extra olive, and sink into the vibe of an almost bygone era.

927 Ninth Ave., 206-397-4053
vitosseattle.com

TIP
Come to Vito's with an empty belly. The food is delicious and, if you get the right table and the right entrée, you'll feel like the world is in the palm of your hand.

LIVE MUSIC
LIKE A LOCAL

While it may seem like there are as many music venues in the city as there are bands, there are a few spots that local music fans especially cherish. If you were to poll everyone who's played a show in the city, it's likely the venue most mentioned as their favorite would be the Tractor Tavern. In a way, it's the exact venue that you'd get if you put the best of all the others in a pot, mixed them around, and *poof!* The Tractor has seen the greats grace its stage—from Pearl Jam to Fiona Apple. The four-hundred-person music club regularly hosts square dance nights, metal nights, rock 'n' roll, and hip-hop shows. It has been home to up-and-coming artists and those in the Rock & Roll Hall of Fame. And it's in the center of Seattle's Ballard neighborhood, a mixture of hard drinkers and vegans.

5213 Ballard Ave. NW, 206-789-3599
tractortavern.com

STAY CLASSY—
AND CLASSICAL

Amidst the grunge music flannel and the black skinny jeans, Seattle makes time for the occasional evening gowns and tailored tuxedos for a night of classical music. Throughout the city, large and elegant concert halls host regular performances of the symphony, opera, and ballet. While there are several options for classical music lovers, we suggest first investigating Benaroya Hall, home of the Seattle Symphony. The imposing glass and stone structure downtown seems more like a monument to performance than any normal bit of architecture. The long hallways lead to a large, red-carpeted lobby, where glasses of wine are sold with spirits to folks in their Sunday best. Inside the 2,500-person hall, some of the world's best players apply their craft to timeless masterpieces in front of a cultured and eager crowd.

200 University St., 206-215-4747
seattlesymphony.org/benaroyahall

RECORD YOUR DEMO
AT SOUNDHOUSE

When you look up through the glass at the engineer on the boards, with your guitar strapped to your shoulder and your pedals at your feet, you are suddenly ready to record the rhythm track. Whether it's a cover song or an original, to record your music in a professional studio while working with other professionals is an unparalleled joy. Listen back to the track to make sure it's just right. Add a bass guitar, drums, piano, or kazoo. In Seattle, there are a plethora of recording studios—and most are of high quality—but at Soundhouse you might get to work with the great engineer Jack Endino, who produced Nirvana's first album, *Bleach*. Endino, perhaps the sincerest man in rock 'n' roll, has won multiple Grammys and has been given the nickname the "Godfather of Grunge." Is there anything cooler than that? Reach the studio through their online contact form to book your session.

Ballard neighborhood
soundhouserecording.net

OTHER PLACES TO TRY

The streaming online music station Hollow Earth Radio offers an eclectic sampling of local tunes, the Columbia City Theater has excellent local music in the city's South End, and Fred Wildlife Refuge in Capitol Hill is a private event space that often offers inventive performances.

Hollow Earth Radio KHUH 104.9 FM
hollowearthradio.org

Columbia City Theater
4916 Rainier Ave. S., 206-722-3009
columbiacitytheater.com

Fred Wildlife Refuge
127 Boylston Ave. E., 206-588-6959
fredwildliferefuge.com

BUT WHERE ARE
ALL THE TOYS?

"No shelf or wall space will go uncovered!" If that's not the official motto of the Greenwood neighborhood's Top Ten Toys, then it should be. The toy store, which is end-to-end games, art supplies, figures, and puzzles, is one of the most exciting places for kids to visit in all of Seattle. As soon as you see the shop's bright yellow sign and colorful logo, something in your heart glimmers, knowing you're about to be surrounded by tools for imagination and fun. While there are educational games, classic toys, and action figures galore, maybe the most lovable area of the store is the stuffed animal aisle, which features pandas, giraffes, seals, and lizards, among many others. It's where wonderment and a good ol' fashioned hug meet in this well-curated toy shop.

120 N. Eighy-Fifth St., 206-782-0098
toptentoys.com

GET READY—
IT'S TIME TO RACE!

It might be the most fun hyphenated word in all of childhood: go-kart. The miniature vehicles provide a rush of speed, demand hand-eye coordination, and, in a philosophical manner, offer a bridge to another era of your life. If you're a kid (without a driving license), go-karts offer the opportunity to sit behind the wheel and show your stuff on the (mostly) open road. If you're an adult and a veteran of the road, sitting in a go-kart can give you back that freedom to weave, wend, and win the race—as opposed to just commute to work again. At Traxx Indoor Raceway, just a twenty-minute drive from Seattle in Mukilteo, all of these thrilling experiences can be yours—and your whole family's, too.

4329 Chennault Beach Rd., Mukilteo, 425-493-8729
traxxracing.com

TAKE A SELFIE
WITH SUPERHEROES

On living room floors right now are countless kids holding their favorite action figures, creating stories with them, pretending to be them. Whether it's a Lego man building a spaceship or Spider-Man slinging his web through the city skyscape, kids love this make-believe. But what if they could walk among giant versions of their favorite figures, some standing even ten feet tall, whenever they wanted? Well, all of this is possible at Funko HQ, which delights with seventeen thousand square feet of retail space and fantastic, immersive scenes inspired by every kid's favorite Marvel, Star Wars, DC Comics, and Harry Potter characters. Imagine, as soon as you walk through the door, that you've shrunk, and now, all of a sudden, you have to joyously make your way between Iron Man and Batgirl to get back to your car.

2802 Wetmore Ave., Everett
funko.com

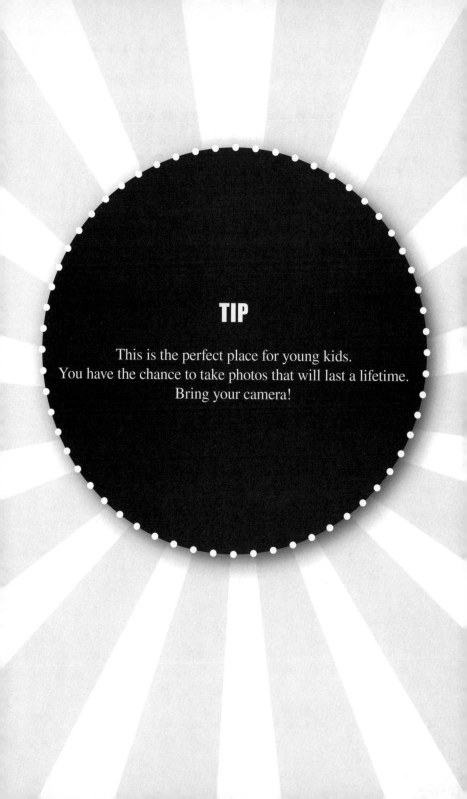

TIP

This is the perfect place for young kids.
You have the chance to take photos that will last a lifetime.
Bring your camera!

IMMERSE YOURSELF
IN THE SEATTLE CHILDREN'S THEATRE

Over the years, going to the theater has become known as some highfalutin objective for the top one percent. But that doesn't have to be the case. In Shakespeare's time, the masses went to see plays. The theater, historically, was the place where the people—of all ages—went to see good, creative entertainment. And at the Seattle Children's Theatre, that remains the case. Nestled in the shadow of the great Space Needle, the Children's Theatre presents some of the city's best actors performing timeless classics like *Where the Wild Things Are, The Little Prince,* and *The Lion, the Witch and the Wardrobe.* If you want your time in the footlights, you can take acting classes at the in-house drama school to perhaps one day be a part of the performance.

201 Thomas St., 206-441-3322
sct.org

ENJOY
BRIGHT LIGHTS AND BIG GAMING

Few things can match the pure, energized excitement that an arcade can manifest in a kid (or a grown-up kid). As soon as you walk into GameWorks in downtown Seattle, the sights and sounds of the arcade make the heart beat faster. Pop-a-shot basketball, behind-the-wheel racecar driving, and many more game options fill the twenty thousand square feet of space. But the thing you can't replicate from the comfort of your living room couch is the spew of tickets that you can trade in for prizes. GameWorks offers 180 games, many of which give back those relished red tickets. And if you get hungry after all your efforts, the arcade offers a restaurant, party rooms, and fifteen TVs to watch the games instead of playing them.

1511 Seventh Ave., 206-521-0952
gameworks.com/locations/seattle-washington

PICK YOUR PLEASURE
AT SUMMER MUSIC FESTIVALS

Perhaps above all else, Seattle is a live music town. Sure, there's coffee, tech, airplanes, and nature, but for as long as the city has been around, nightlife and live music have been a part of it. And at no time is this more evident than during the summer months. From May through September, there are more music festivals than any sane person can keep track of. But for the purposes of this book, we'll try. For a smaller, curated experience, check out Timber! in pastoral Carnation. For a large (free!) community festival, check out the Northwest Folklife Festival in Seattle Center. To see some of the biggest names in music, don't miss Sasquatch! at the Gorge Amphitheatre in George. In Seattle, Bumbershoot and the Capitol Hill Block Party offer similar high-level talent within the city limits throughout the warm months. If you want your music to be accompanied by a naked bike ride, be sure to enjoy the Fremont Summer Solstice, or if you want to camp out in the woods with music-loving hippies, mellow out at the Summer Meltdown Festival in Darrington.

visitseattle.org/things-to-do/events/festivals/

EAT LUNCH
TO A TUNE

If you're ever downtown during the summer months around lunchtime, you're probably going to catch the faraway sound of a song. In 2017 the Downtown Seattle Association hosted forty-seven lunchtime shows featuring local artists like the prolific and unabashed rock 'n' roll guitar player Ayron Jones and the funky and soulful neo-jazz band Industrial Revelation. The summer shows, which only last about as long as it takes you to eat lunch, bring the city's downtown to life. People of all ages hang out on the Harbor Steps or in other locations around the city and listen to independent music—one of Seattle's most prized products. They can eat a slice of pizza or falafel from a nearby food truck and remember what it is to be a tried-and-true Seattleite.

downtownseattle.org/events/out-to-lunch/

SPORTS AND RECREATION

BE THE TWELFTH MAN
WITH THE SEATTLE SEAHAWKS

Before each game, a local celebrity raises the giant "12" flag, and the crowd erupts in CenturyLink Field. The past five years have been especially passionate for 'Hawks fans. The city has seen the team win a Super Bowl and, the following year, make the worst play in Super Bowl history and go on to lose the game. During those years, the Seahawks have also produced many memorable players, including Richard Sherman, Russell Wilson, Marshawn Lynch, and a slew of All-Pro defensive players. The team is the hottest ticket in town, and while they always face some offseason question marks, the city is so invested in the 'Hawks that fans are sure to follow every move. As the city has continued to grow, the Seahawks have remained one of the most common talking points, proving yet again that sports can be a bond for a community.

800 Occidental Ave. S., 206-381-7555
centurylinkfield.com

CHOW DOWN
WITH THE MARINERS

As the sun sets and you take a bite of your second hot dog, you realize the serenity of baseball that the great writers described at the turn of the twentieth century. There's majesty to baseball, coupled with a calm glory and a sense of wonderment. While Seattle's team hasn't been much good—save for one magical season in 2001—since the glory days of the great Ken Griffey Jr., catching a game is still one of the best summertime activities in the city. Safeco Field, which hosted its first baseball game July 15, 1999, remains one of the most beautiful parks in major league baseball, and because Seattle is such a food- and craft beer-centric city, the refreshments at the park are always delicious. And some snacks, like the fried grasshoppers, even wow the most courageous eater. But if food isn't your thing, you can enjoy every kind of beer from Bud Light to a locally brewed IPA as you watch "King" Félix Hernández strike out another batter.

1250 First Ave. S., 206-346-4000
mlb.com/mariners/ballpark

TIP
Safeco Field is one of the best places in the city to go for a stroll. You'll find excellent people watching, delicious food, and a great drink selection. Oh, and there's a professional baseball game going on at the same time.

SCORE YOUR LIFE GOALS
WITH THE SEATTLE SOUNDERS

The rumble only gets louder. As you walk the catacombs of CenturyLink Field, the sound of the crowd rises and rises. Seattle is notorious for its boisterous fans, especially when it comes to the city's beloved Seattle Sounders. Led by a mix of veterans like Clint Dempsey and young talent like Jordan Morris, the team has continued to pique the city's interest, often playing deep into the playoffs, and even winning the MLS Cup in 2016. While the country at large hasn't quite taken to soccer like the Pacific Northwest has—the Sounders have a heated rivalry with southern neighbor the Portland Timbers—Seattle has embraced the squad with open arms. Tens of thousands pack each game, wildly cheering while waving signature green scarves.

800 Occidental Ave. S., 206-381-7555
centurylinkfield.com

CHEER A SSSSWWIIIISSHHHH
WITH THE STORM

Ask any Seattleite their thoughts on the NBA, and they'll grimace and probably curse David Stern, the former league commissioner who sold off the city's Seattle SuperSonics. But while Stern is the villain, Dawn Trudeau and her Force 10 ownership group are heroes. The NBA team left in the dark of night for parts unknown (or at least unacknowledged), but the WNBA team, the Seattle Storm, stayed in the Emerald City and continues to provide fans with high-level basketball and captivating competition. Some of women's basketball's greatest players have donned a Storm uniform, including Sue Bird and Swin Cash. A Seattle Storm game, played in KeyArena, is a great family outing. Experience the joy of professional hoops while crunching on popcorn and intermittently admiring the Storm's championship banners from 2004 and 2010.

305 Harrison St., 206-684-7200
keyarena.com

TIP
You might be amazed at how quickly you become invested in the game. Bring an extra twenty dollars for a Storm souvenir to commemorate your new love after the final buzzer.

DO LITERALLY EVERYTHING
AT ROXBURY LANES

Let's say you're in your living room with your spouse and kids and you ask, "What does everyone want to do today?" Someone says bowling, another says the arcade, the third is hungry, and you, of course, want to play a few hands of cards. Oh, cruel world! But wait, there's a solution: Roxbury Lanes. There are entertainment options for everyone inside White Center's one-stop fun center, which includes about a dozen bowling lanes, a classic arcade room equipped with air hockey and pop-a-shot basketball, a restaurant serving Chinese food and Americana favorites, and a card room where locals legally play. There may be no other place on earth where you can get fried rice, bowl a strike, play Pac-Man, and win on a royal flush.

2823 SW Roxbury St., 206-935-7400
roxburylanesbowl.com

HAVE DINNER
AND A MOVIE ... THEATER

It takes a magical place to offer all that Central Cinema does. On one night, the movie theater might show *Labyrinth,* starring David Bowie. On another, it might feature Ryan Reynolds in *Deadpool.* And no matter what classic or contemporary movie might be showing, ticketholders can order snacks like pigs in a blanket, kale salad with golden raisins, and, of course, popcorn with either butter, curry powder, or cinnamon sugar. For dinner, the house offers items like hamburgers, field roast burgers, meatballs and gravy, gnocchi in wild mushroom cream sauce, and a handful of pizzas, including one with pear and Gorgonzola. With a carefully curated list of films, the cozy movie theater is the perfect place to lose yourself in good food and a satisfying story for a few hours.

1411 Twenty-First Ave., 206-328-3230
central-cinema.com

TIP
Check the listings at Central Cinema; sometimes there are really fun movie trivia sessions during which winners receive cheesy VHS tapes as prizes for their efforts.

BACKWARDS SKATE
AT SKATE KING

Pull up your rainbow socks and put on your most ironic T-shirt because it's time to lace up some roller skates and remember what it was like when weekend fun didn't include cell phones, Facebook invitations, or streaming music—a time when you made a plan to meet your friends at the roller rink and you stuck to it. At Skate King, the DJ in the booth controls the jams, and the fun is had in circles, whether it's couple's skate, backwards skate, or doing the hokey pokey with two dozen strangers, turning yourself around. And, if you get tired of skating, the nostalgic spot offers a snack bar and giant sodas, an arcade with classic games, and the tricky crane game where you can win that special someone a stuffed penguin.

14326 124th Ave. NE, Kirkland, 425-254-8750
snokingkirkland.com

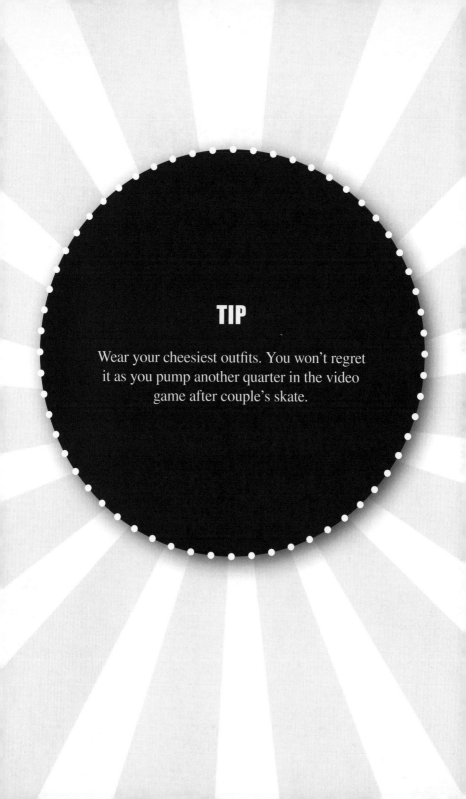

TIP

Wear your cheesiest outfits. You won't regret
it as you pump another quarter in the video
game after couple's skate.

HIT THE PEAK
OF THE REI PINNACLE

From I-5, passing between Eastlake and Queen Anne, REI looks like a challenge. The giant outdoors store beckons like the curling index finger from a coach who knows just what to do to get you in shape. Looking upon it, it's as if the store is saying, "Get moving!" One of the most enticing aspects of the shop, besides its myriad shoes, outerwear, and gear, is the giant climbing wall known as the REI Climbing Pinnacle, a sixty-five-foot-tall structure that the not-so-faint-of-heart can reserve to try out their new shoes or their fortitude. Those who reach the top are treated to expansive views of the city, and you may even catch a glimpse of Mount Rainier, which might in fact be your next challenge.

222 Yale Ave. N., 206-223-1944
rei.com/stores/seattle.html

EXPLORE
THE BURKE-GILMAN TRAIL

Begin your morning at Recycled Cycles, which is located right on the edge of Portage Bay. The quintessential bike shop—where all the staff members cycle in their free time and wear bike gloves to work—will equip you with a rented ride, along with helmet and lock, for your trek up the twenty-seven-mile Burke-Gilman Trail. When you've gotten your ride, pedal along the route heading northeast. If your legs stay with you, travel the whole hour and a half and hit the Chateau Ste. Michelle Winery, which stands right off the trail. Or, if you can't muster that much strength, hit any of the pubs and restaurants along the way, including the nearby McMenamins Anderson School, which offers eats and libations in the neighboring town of Bothell.

Burke-Gilman Trail
traillink.com/trail/burke-gilman-trail

Recycled Cycles
1007 NE Boat St., 206-547-4491
recycledcycles.com

McMenamins Anderson School
18607 Bothell Way NE, Bothell, 425-398-0122
mcmenamins.com/anderson-school

BRUSH UP
ON YOUR CURLING

Every four years, during the Winter Olympics, half the world goes, "Ohhh, yeaaahh! Curling!" Well, the sport, which involves sending a thick stone disk down a straight sheet of ice, is never forgotten in the Emerald City, thanks to the Granite Curling Club. At the club, surefooted athletes, who don't mind the ice and a little chill, practice the art of hitting the bullseye, known as the "house"—or knocking their opponents from the bullseye—from 150 feet away with the forty-pound-plus stone. Players can take lessons, join leagues, or just come for pick-up games. Curling, which was invented in Scotland and is similar to bowling or shuffleboard, has been around for more than five hundred years. And thanks to the Granite Curling Club (and yes, the Winter Olympics, too), it is sure to be around many more.

1440 N. 128th St., 206-362-2446
curlingseattle.org

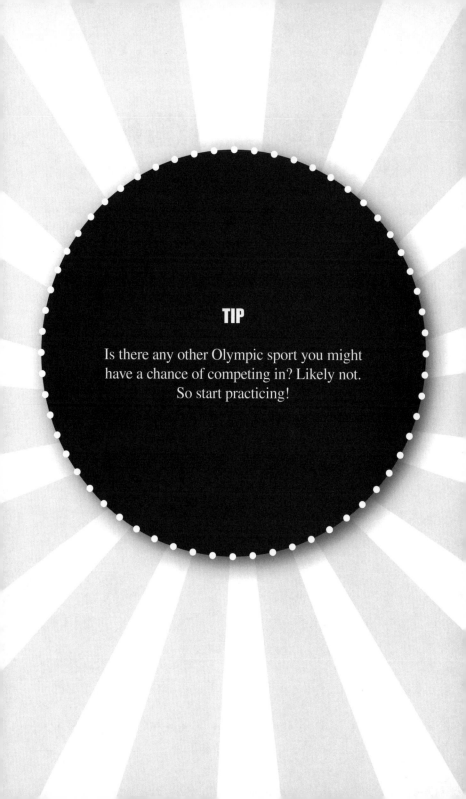

TIP

Is there any other Olympic sport you might have a chance of competing in? Likely not. So start practicing!

ROW THROUGH
LILY PADS AND FLOATING HOUSES

Nestled beside Seattle's glistening Portage Bay, Agua Verde Café and Paddle Club offers kayaking and stand-up paddleboarding rentals to those looking to bob on luxurious, diamond-crisp waters. Strap on your puffy life vest and slide just so into a boat, solo or with a friend, to explore the waterways from Agua Verde's dock to Gas Works Park and beyond. Or go the other direction and wend under highways and find the lily pads on the east side of the bay. Either way, on your journey you'll see yachts, motorboats, and people along the shore waving hello. And afterwards, upon returning your gear, stop into the adjoining café for tacos or a quesadilla to recount all that you saw and wonder, checking your phone, how much it might cost to buy or rent out one of those floating homes.

1303 NE Boat St., 206-545-8570 x101
aguaverde.com

ATTEMPT DOWNWARD DOG
ON A PADDLEBOARD

In the middle of Green Lake, one of the most picturesque areas in all of Seattle, those in need of physical and mental serenity can rent paddleboards from SUP Yoga, get on the water, and follow live instruction with other like-minded folks who are practicing the ancient Indian art. Green Lake, which is surrounded by a 2.8-mile path frequented by walkers and stroller pushers, is home to cafés, restaurants, and running stores of all kinds. It's a local mecca for fitness—including the floating yoga classes—and those seeking a refined but natural experience. Instruction is offered mornings and evenings and challenges even the most seasoned yogis to maintain balance as swans, ducks, and turtles swim nearby. After the class, with your stomach grumbling, there are plenty of eateries to satiate your spiritually induced hunger.

7351 East Green Lake Dr. N., 206-605-3737
supyogaseattle.com

DROP THE GLOVES
WITH THE THUNDERBIRDS

They say hockey is the most exciting sport to watch live. And perhaps the most exciting form of hockey is minor league. The players are young, hungry, and itching for their chance to hit the NHL. Founded in 1985, the Seattle Thunderbirds, officially a "major junior ice hockey team," have made their mark on the Emerald City, making the finals of their league most recently in 2015. Playing in Kent at the ShoWare Center, the Thunderbirds, who have sent a handful of players to the NHL, are inspiring a new wave of hockey fans. And while Seattle loves the team, many are also hoping for a bona fide NHL squad. Some local elites, including big-time hedge-fund manager Chris Hansen, are pushing for a glitzy professional squad. In the meantime, though, it's a Thunderbirds kind of town.

625 W. James St., Kent, 253-856-6777
accessoshowarecenter.com

SEE SEATTLE
FROM THE UNDERGROUND

Seattle is known as one of the smartest cities in the country. It's a tech center and is regularly voted as the most literate city in the United States. But you can judge for yourself whether the decision made by city officials in the late nineteenth century to rebuild Seattle on top of itself after a giant fire was particularly bright or not. Yes, in 1889, after a terrible fire, the city, instead of clearing all the rubble, just built on top of it. But a portion of the forgotten town remains and can be toured to this day. Seattle's Underground Tour, which begins in Pioneer Square at Pioneer Place Park, is a seventy-five-minute (humorous) exploration of hidden tunnels, subterranean storefronts, and sidewalks preserved from Seattle's earliest days when it was a logging outpost at the end of the country.

614 First Ave., 206-682-4646
undergroundtour.com

GET SCARED
BY GHOSTS

Each year, millions of people go and see scary movies in the theater to experience a bit of fright and feel that chill crawl up their spine. Those ghosts are fake and generated by computers, but in Seattle, those interested in a little scare can get a couple of tickets to a haunted tour of Seattle and maybe see the real thing. In association with AGHOST (Advanced Ghost Hunters of Seattle–Tacoma), the Spooked in Seattle Tours have been investigating the paranormal in the city and telling the tales of those who might be lingering a little too long. Founded in 2001, AGHOST says they're the oldest paranormal investigation team in the Pacific Northwest. They offer a Pioneer Square Ghost Tour and a Haunted Pub Tour to go along with their Death Museum, for the supremely curious.

102 Cherry St., 425-954-7701
spookedinseattle.squarespace.com

CONTROL THE CHAOS
WITH THE RAT CITY ROLLERGIRLS

The thing about a roller derby is that you've never seen anything like it. It's a constant scrum of competition swirling around an oval rink, where two teams are vying for mental and physical domination. It's a dervish, a Tasmanian Devil-ish brawl with battles both individual and team within the bout. The Rat City Roller Derby (formerly the Rat City Rollergirls), an all-female squad that started in 2004, plays its home bouts at The Rat's Nest. The team, which shares its nickname with the South End's White Center neighborhood, schedules around ten bouts a year for its team of about ten players. Traditionally, the Roller Derby athletes have been formidable—so much so that they often motivate youngsters to take up the sport. So get ready to get inspired!

19022 Aurora Ave. N., Shoreline, 206-599-9613
ratcityrollergirls.com

WALK
WITH THE ANIMALS

Hanging there in the corner of a big glass window is a sloth. You may have seen sloths in cartoons; you may have seen them in internet memes. But here one is, in real life, right in front of you. It hangs casually, smiling away, probably daydreaming about its next meal or its next nap. And right beside the sloth's, um, hangout is a window into the den of a giant Komodo dragon, stretched out by a log. And you say to yourself, "Wow! That's a giant Komodo dragon!" At the Woodland Park Zoo, you can see creatures of all kinds, from tigers to colorful birds to elephants, and if you were to visit during winter, you could also catch the beloved WildLights display, an array of beautifully curated holiday lights.

5500 Phinney Ave. N., 206-548-2500
zoo.org

PEAK
YOUR INTEREST

Quick—imagine the biggest thing you can think of. Okay? Well, you probably couldn't, off the top of your head, picture something that's 235,625 acres. That's how big Mount Rainier National Park is. The park, which gets about 1.5 million visitors per year, is home to more wildlife than most people will see in a lifetime—from black bears and mountain goats to the small, adorable looks-like-a-mouse-but-is-actually-more-like-a-bunny pika, not to mention multitudes of birds, reptiles, fish, and other critters. Visitors can admire the scenic views, hike around the designated natural areas, or snowshoe up the iconic, looming mountain that most locals only dare admire from afar. While permits aren't required for day hiking, if you'd like to camp overnight at the park, you must make provisions. Explore more than three dozen trails while admiring all that grows among the natural majesty. And, if you find yourself at the base of a waterfall, remember one thing: paradise actually does exist for some.

360-569-2211
nps.gov/mora/index.htm

PLUNGE INTO THE SEA
AT THE SEATTLE AQUARIUM

It seems almost fantastical to think you'd be able to see a starfish up close. They're more like made-up cartoon creatures—like a coyote that can order things from ACME—than real, live organisms that grow and procreate. But at the Seattle Aquarium, you can see starfish—not to mention sea otters, octopuses, turtles, and myriad fish—up close like you were Jacques Cousteau. The aquarium, which is great for a visually stunning visit or to learn about nature and ocean conservation, is located on Pier 59, not far from downtown and Pike Place Market. And the place is so enchanting that it even hosts weddings among the tanks of cool blue water and slowly swimming sea creatures.

Pier 59
1483 Alaskan Way, 206-386-4300
seattleaquarium.org

OTHER PLACES TO TRY

Looking for a good game? At Capitol Hill's
Cal Anderson Park, there are regular pick-up games
of soccer, baseball, tennis, and basketball. Or, if
you're looking to swim but it's raining outside,
check out the Evans Pool in Green Lake or the
Ballard Pool in Ballard.

Cal Anderson Park
1635 Eleventh Ave., 206-684-4075
seattle.gov/parks/find/parks/cal-anderson-park

Evans Pool
7201 East Green Lake Dr. N., 206-684-4961
seattle.gov/parks/find/pools/evans-pool

Ballard Pool
1471 NW Sixty-Seventh St., 206-684-4094
seattle.gov/parks/find/pools/ballard-pool

SKYDIVE
WITHOUT A PLANE

For many of us, no amount of money would be enough to get in a plane, attach a parachute to our backs and, some twenty thousand feet later, jump out into the open sky with faith on our side. But that's exactly why the good people at iFLY Indoor Skydiving exist: to give you the thrill of falling through the air at 120 miles per hour without actually taking any risk. With the friendly help of an instructor, you strap into your jumpsuit and, as the air rushes by faster and faster, you're guided on balance and movement strategies amid the oncoming rush, while you're suspended horizontally in mid-air by giant rushes from a wind chamber. With a few solid lessons, you'll quickly mimic the instructors, doing back and front flips like a dolphin in the ocean.

349 Tukwila Pkwy., Tukwila, 206-244-4359
iflyworld.com/seattle

SWING THROUGH THE AIR
IN BELLEVUE

You may not need any extra incentive to fly through the air, but at the Bellevue Zip Tour, you can do so through lush forest greenery along the hundreds of feet of zip lines as if you're Tarzan or Spider-Man, on lines seventy-six to 450 feet in length. People aged nine and up will don gloves, a helmet, and giant grins as they soar from platform to platform up to eighty feet in the air amidst Douglas firs and broadleaf maple trees. Each zip tour can accommodate up to ten riders, and prices range from fifty-three dollars for kids to seventy-eight dollars for adults—a small pittance when facing the proposition of being a tree ninja for a few hours!

14509 SE Newport Way, 425-452-7101
bellevueziptour.com

ENJOY
BUMPER BOATS, BOWLING, AND HAMBURGERS!

If you were asked to rattle off all the things you'd need to create the perfect amusement park, you'd likely only be able to come up with a portion of what's possible at the Family Fun Center. Laser tag, go-karts, mini golf, roller coaster-like swings, batting cages, bumper cars AND bumper boats, and the human slingshot are just some of the options for the whole family. No matter the weather, the size of your party, or the level of adventure you're seeking, there is plenty to do at the Family Fun Center. Or maybe your thing is to bowl a few frames and then grab some fries with a delicious hamburger. That too is a possibility in the place where just about everything is possible.

7300 Fun Center Way, Tukwila, 425-228-7300
fun-center.com/tukwila

EXPLORE AND CLIMB

When the idea of a sprawling amusement park isn't your top choice, but you need something to bring a little joy to the family, the eight-thousand-square-foot PlayDate SEA is a terrific choice. Featuring interactive dance floors, climbing, crawling, and many other movement-based activities, the park has separate toddler areas for the very young, and parents are encouraged to play right along with the kids (with no additional fee). Open seven days a week, PlayDate SEA also offers puppet shows, laser tag, and a café with meals for both kids and adults. Explore plastic tunnels and slides, climb over obstacles, and put a smile back on the faces of the entire family. To finish the day off, try a slice of pizza that could satisfy a famished soldier's hunger.

1275 Mercer St., 206-623-7529
playdatesea.com

OTHER PLACES TO TRY

Along with many kid-friendly activities, try some of Seattle's kid-friendly restaurants, including the Ballard Pizza Company Frelard and Vios Café, both of which have kid play areas for diners.

Ballard Pizza Company Frelard
4010 Leary Way NW, 206-946-9966
ballardpizzacompany.com

Vios Café
903 Nineteenth Ave. E., 206-329-3236
vioscafe.com

SEE A WHALE— GUARANTEED!

A few hours outside the Emerald City is the small ferry town of Anacortes. It has its own brewery, a few good restaurants (shout out to the A-Town Bistro!), and during the summer, it's home to one of the most experienced and enjoyable whale-watching tours in the area. Island Adventures guarantees that its passengers see a whale— and they know just where to look. With boats leaving regularly throughout the day during the summery months (i.e., March through October), captains know how to spot bald eagles, minke whales, and the big guys: humpbacks or killer whales. With more than one hundred years of combined experience maneuvering through the islands, the crew has led people to thousands and thousands of whale sightings. And you could be next.

1801 Commercial Ave., Anacortes, 360-293-2428
island-adventures.com

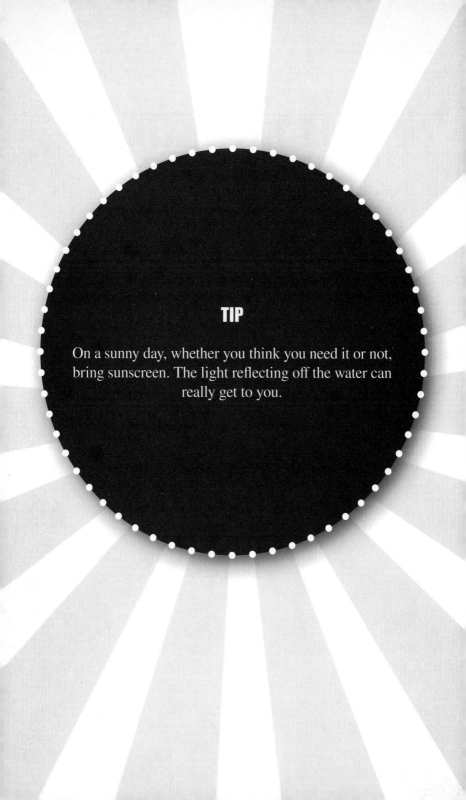

TIP

On a sunny day, whether you think you need it or not, bring sunscreen. The light reflecting off the water can really get to you.

FLY YOUR KITE
AT GAS WORKS PARK

If you were to fly over the entire city of Seattle, you would see lots of impressive skyscrapers, lovely residential neighborhoods, beautiful green spaces, and water—lots of water. You would see the iconic, hip-retro Space Needle, and then you would notice a rusted, rambling collection of pipes and towers that resemble some giant gadget out of a steampunk fantasy. This is Gas Works Park. Located on the north shore of Lake Union at the south side of the Wallingford neighborhood, the 19.1-acre Gas Works Park, centered around a former coal gasification plant operated by the city of Seattle, has become synonymous with outdoor enjoyment in this city. Lie on a towel and soak up the rays or fly a kite from the top of the Great Mound, a pile of rubble from the plant covered over with soil and topped with a fantastical sun dial.

2101 N. Northlake Way, 206-684-4075
seattle.gov/parks/find/parks/gas-works-park

TAKE FLIGHT
IN A SEATTLE SEAPLANE

Anyone who's been near the Eastlake neighborhood in Seattle during the sunny months has admired a thick-winged, bobbing seaplane floating on the water of Lake Union. If they watch long enough, the seaplane will rev its engines, flit across the water, and take off, almost magically, lifting into the air and circling the sky before zipping off to some other location. It's an enviable spectacle and one many want to try. And you can, at Seattle Seaplanes. See the city from the cockpit of a tiny plane. Fly higher than the top of the Space Needle, be one with the crows and seagulls, and then touch down like a goose hitting the tops of the diamond waves. It's a rare and exhilarating experience that costs less than one hundred dollars per passenger and covers more than thirty miles in about twenty minutes, with views of the university, downtown, the floating bridges, and many more notable sights.

1325 Fairview Ave. E., 206-329-9638
seattleseaplanes.com

WATCH YOUR FAVORITE MOVIE ... OUTSIDE

During the summer months, the Seattle Summer Outdoor Movie Series showcases cult classics, pop favorites, and the most beloved all-time greats throughout many of the Emerald City's popular neighborhoods. Broadcast on giant screens or on the sides of buildings from Fremont to Westlake Park to the City Center Mural, movies like *Star Wars, The Princess Bride,* and many other favorites entertain audiences of all ages. To enjoy the nights at their fullest, we suggest you pack a picnic blanket, snacks, pillows, and maybe a bottle of wine—and then recline and enjoy. They say, in spite of a million entertainment options at home, that it's the communal experiences we love most. So relax and watch *The Goonies* with a couple hundred of your closest friends in the warm, fleeting, Seattle summer night.

See seattlemet.com for schedules and locations.

FIND YOURSELF
ON A BOAT!

Because Seattle is surrounded by water, people who live in the city have the great pleasure of hopping on a boat by foot or with vehicle and traveling to countless islands around the metropolis. From Whidbey to the San Juans and even to Canada via the *Victoria Clipper* to have tea or walk through a rose garden, you will find an abundance of travel options by water. And while the *Clipper* may take a few hours to get to our neighbor in the north, some of the ferry trips are short enough that, after a soft pretzel and cheese from the onboard cage and a game of Go Fish, you'll be where you want to be—ready to step ashore again, after navigating the glinting waters, to shop, visit a new brewery, or go wine tasting.

2711 Alaskan Way, 1-800-888-2535
clippervacations.com

RELISH THE VIEW
THROUGH THE TREES

If you find yourself stressed with city life, there are other options. No, you don't have to travel to the mountains or hop a plane for the middle of Alaska. In Seattle, much like New York City, there is significant land set aside for green space and parks. Nearly every neighborhood has its own park, or multiple parks, where residents can walk their dog, lay out on the grass, or play hopscotch. Some are just big enough for a few benches and a slide. But others, like Discovery Park, are huge, lush, and diverse—you can walk flights of stairs between the trees, find yourself on the beach, or get lost for miles among all the pathways. It's the perfect place for some fresh air and to move those muscles.

3801 Discovery Park Blvd., 206-684-4075
seattle.gov/parks/find/parks/discovery-park

RIDE.
THE. GREAT. WHEEL.

"Come one, come all! See the city from the top of the Great Wheel!" And indeed you can. Standing 175 feet tall on Elliott Bay's Pier 57, not far from Pike Place Market, the Seattle Great Wheel is magnificent, especially during the summer. Whether it's lit up in a multitude of colors to celebrate the Fourth of July or a recent Mariners win or is just shining with a brilliant golden glow, the giant Ferris wheel makes for the perfect exclamation point to a first date or a new way to take a look at the beautiful Emerald City spread out beneath you. It was the tallest Ferris wheel on the West Coast when it was unveiled June 29, 2012, and it still presides with elegance and class over downtown. Each of the wheel's gondolas can hold eight people—but they may in fact be best suited for two lovebirds.

Pier 57
1301 Alaskan Way, 206-623-8607
seattlegreatwheel.com

CARRY NO CARES
AT SEAFAIR

It never fails—whenever it's Seafair Weekend in Seattle, the weather couldn't be better and the sun couldn't be shinier. Somehow the gods just know. Ever since 1950, Seafair Weekend brings to the city boat racing on sparkling water, the impossible-not-to-notice Blue Angels soaring acrobatically through the sky, and lots of ocean-bred fare. But even more than any particular activity, the weekend is a chance for Seattle to embrace the rays like no other time during the calendar year. It's the time the most tank tops, bathing suits, sunglasses, and sunscreen are worn by a long shot. It's the weekend we get to feel like we're Florida for a couple of afternoons, and it's just the mood for cheap beer and loud music. Plus boats.

2200 Sixth Ave., Ste. 400 (corporate office), 206-728-0123
seafair.com

TIP
Drink water. Lots of it.

HIT
THE BEACH!

Seattle summers are like an oasis shimmering in the sight of the world's thirstiest man—a long-hoped-for, but barely imagined, treasure. It can get so dreary during the winter that sunlight, when available, seems like a lifesaver. And one of the most popular ways to celebrate the sun in Seattle is to go to the beach. There are several well-trodden options for sunbathing on sand by the water, including Madison and Matthews beaches, but the two most beloved have to be Alki and Golden Gardens. Alki is a 136-acre park and beach in West Seattle overlooking Elliott Bay. It's a popular hangout for dog walkers, volleyball players, and restaurant-goers. Golden Gardens hosts regular cookouts and acoustic band performances and has that California beach quality that maybe no other place in the city can claim.

Alki Beach Park
1702 Alki Ave. SW, 206-684-4075
seattle.gov/parks/find/parks/alki-beach-park

Golden Gardens Park
8498 Seaview Pl. NW, 206-684-4075
seattle.gov/parks/find/parks/golden-gardens-park

MEANDER THROUGH TIME
AT A TIMELESS SEATTLE WATERWAY

Officially dubbed the Hiram M. Chittenden Locks—but much better known as the Ballard Locks—this picturesque area in the western part of the city represents an early era of Seattle, one that remains supremely necessary but is more and more overlooked as the city continues its bend toward high tech, food, and beverage as cultural mainstays. The locks, which link Puget Sound with Lake Union and Lake Washington, are a place where boaters can commune and larger ships can deliver cargo. The area, which opened in 1917, is also a regular place for tourists to walk among the natural beauty, see the salmon swimming by, and watch the boats traverse the waves.

3015 NW Fifty-Fourth St., 206-783-7059 (Visitor Center)
nws.usace.army.mil/Missions/Civil-Works/Locks-and-Dams/
Chittenden-Locks

REMEMBER,
THE WORLD IS STILL A LOVELY PLACE

One huge benefit to Seattle's incessant precipitation during much of the year is the lush greenery and widespread flora that pops up everywhere throughout the city. It can feel like you're walking through a rain forest sometimes just getting from your apartment to the corner store. And there are places in the city where this abundant beauty is concentrated and cultivated in stunning ways. Two gardens visitors to Seattle should check out are the Washington Park Arboretum and the Japanese Garden. The arboretum is a lovely encapsulation of Northwest grandeur all the way down to its famed azaleas. And the Japanese Garden transports you to a place that values above all else the precise expression of what's beautiful in the world.

Washington Park Arboretum
2300 Arboretum Dr. E., 206-543-8800
botanicgardens.uw.edu/washington-park-arboretum

Japanese Garden
1075 Lake Washington Blvd. E., 206-684-4725
seattlejapanesegarden.org

CULTURE AND HISTORY

TAKE A
WRITING CLASS
FROM A WORLD-CLASS POET

In 2018, Seattle staple Hugo House has changed homes. For many years, the creaky old building stained with wine and shaped by history stood in the center of the popular Capitol Hill neighborhood. With the changing city landscape, the building, which offers writing classes and readings galore, had to move. Now, Hugo House resides in a newer, sturdier building that's more equipped to handle significant foot traffic. While the new location will host many more readings in its larger auditorium, the real charm of the place is knowing that in Seattle, Hugo House will maintain its stead as one of the country's strongest literary hubs, continuing a literature tradition that has benefited so many in the city, from student to professional.

1021 Columbia St., 206-322-7030
hugohouse.org

TIP

Hugo House is a must-visit for any trip to the Emerald City. Whether catching a reading, taking a class, or visiting for a lecture, the place will enliven your creative spirit.

TAKE IN
A PLAY

Something special happens when you put on your fancy clothes, link arms with someone you love, and head to the theater. Whether you're off to see a Sherlock Holmes mystery, a James Baldwin narrative, or a work from an up-and-coming playwright you've never heard of, sitting in those rows of people and watching a story come to life is transporting. Seattle is lucky to be home to a wide variety of theaters, but two of the best are ACT—A Contemporary Theatre and the Intiman Theatre. While ACT specializes in both performance and one-on-one interviews throughout the year, the Intiman focuses its efforts on the theater's annual summer festival, a collection of works from authors like local writer Dan Savage to luminaries like Tennessee Williams.

ACT—A Contemporary Theatre
700 Union St., 206-292-7676
acttheatre.org

Intiman Theatre
Various venues, 206-441-7178
intiman.org

SEE PRICELESS ART
AT THE SAM

Outside the Seattle Art Museum stands a giant black metal sculpture of a man hammering away on a project. *Hammering Man,* by Jonathan Borofsky, tirelessly travails outside of one of the most creative hubs in the city. The SAM, as it's affectionately known, holds priceless works of art on its multiple floors and also hosts regular exhibits by internationally acclaimed artists—like a recent show with artist Yayoi Kusama called *Infinity Mirrors,* which showcased an expanse of shimmering wonder that never seemed to end. But the museum's myriad exhibitions include pieces from all over the world, like wooden African masks, Asian statues, ancient Mediterranean coins, Native American sculpture, and European landscapes and portraits. While it's the kind of place you want to take your family for a thoughtful Saturday afternoon, it's also the perfect place for a little culture on your lunch break.

1300 First Ave., 206-654-3100
seattleartmuseum.org

BECOME A
PINBALL (MUSEUM) WIZARD

Close your eyes and imagine as many pinball machines as you possibly can. Done? Well, the Seattle Pinball Museum has even more than that—fifty-plus machines that rotate in and out of row upon row of gaming fun. For decades, Seattle has remained a hub of pinball, although admittedly, the game had to hang on by the skin of its teeth. Today, pinball is experiencing a renaissance, and it's thanks in part to this museum. With games from as early as 1934, the museum allows pinball lovers and collectors to play these antique machines that are still in pristine condition. And, if you get peckish during your visit, the museum serves vintage sodas, craft beers, and tasty snacks. So become part of this burgeoning tradition and play like a pinball wizard.

508 Maynard Ave. S., 206-623-0759
seattlepinballmuseum.com

TIP

You don't even need quarters! One admission fee allows you to play all you want from open to close.

WALK
OLYMPIC SCULPTURE PARK

Along the ocean's waterline, not far from historic Pike Place Market, runs a branch of Seattle Art Museum that provides a walk among brilliant works of art with a stunning view all around. Olympic Sculpture Park is an adventure through nature, art, and your own imagination. Open thirty minutes prior to sunrise and closed thirty minutes after sunset, the park weaves together dozens of expertly crafted sculptures that lure you along step after step. It's as if you're walking in a fantasyland, and then all of a sudden, a giant red iron creature shows itself from behind a tree trunk, bending in the grass before you. During the summer months, the park regularly features standout performances from local bands as food trucks accompany this beautiful and artful experience.

2901 Western Ave., 206-654-3100
seattleartmuseum.org/visit/olympic-sculpture-park

BE ONE
WITH THE CELESTIAL UNIVERSE

While it may be an easy thing to put your eye to a telescope and see the stars out the other end, it's a rare thing that can make you feel like you've been shot suddenly from the face of the earth into the stars themselves. At the palatial Pacific Science Center, you can, in one moment, behold the broad view from the IMAX Theaters, seeing what a mosquito looks like magnified a bajillion times or viewing the fiery surface of the sun. In another moment, you can be in the laser dome, seeing what it's like to match neon blazes of light with some of the city's best musicians. Or in the science center itself, you can tell exactly how big a dinosaur is by standing next to one.

200 Second Ave. N., 206-443-2001
pacificsciencecenter.org

EXPERIENCE GLASS DREAMSCAPES
WITH CHIHULY

From a distance, they look like drawings. Up close? Candy. The colorful, dynamic artwork of Dale Chihuly has traversed the world. But the Seattle-based artist's work can always be seen underneath the Space Needle at Chihuly Garden and Glass. There, you walk through about a dozen rooms—stopping, if you wish, to watch a few short documentaries about the artist's creative process—taking in the sometimes under-the-sea, sometimes on-the-red-planet, and sometimes volcanic-looking creations from the imaginative Emerald City native. Admire the giant blown cylinders or the intricately woven arms that Chihuly creates, along with his network of employees, so effortlessly and prolifically. And, afterwards, sit and chat with a friend in the adjoining café about your artistic opinions on the internationally acclaimed art.

305 Harrison St., 206-753-4940
chihulygardenandglass.com

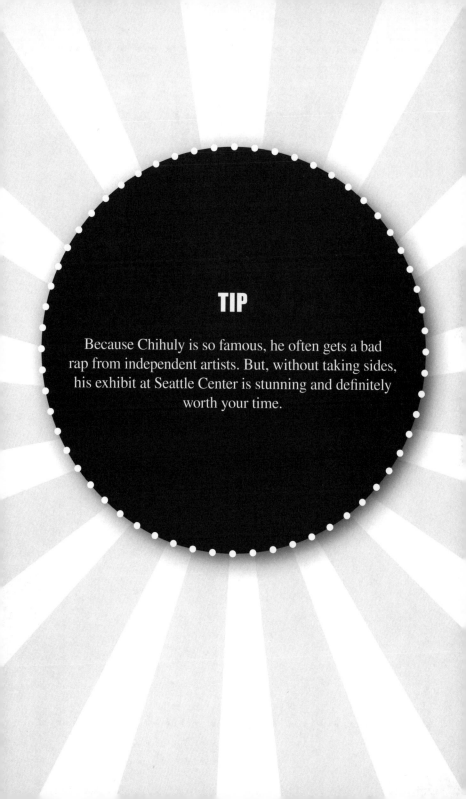

TIP

Because Chihuly is so famous, he often gets a bad rap from independent artists. But, without taking sides, his exhibit at Seattle Center is stunning and definitely worth your time.

CHERISH
THE ARTIFACTS OF POP CULTURE ON DISPLAY

A jacket that belonged to Jimi Hendrix. A smashed guitar played by Kurt Cobain. Miss Piggy's best pink dress. These are but some of the amazing pieces of pop culture that you can see with your own eyes at the Museum of Pop Culture. Created by Microsoft cofounder Paul Allen, MoPop's exterior is a shimmery metallic silver that you can see from miles away. But its interior is a vast display of fun objects sourced from the country's favorite TV, movie, and mainstream pop culture characters. Whether you're wanting to see Spock's uniform from *Star Trek,* the original Hello Kitty artwork, or the exact cut of cloth on The Flash's jumpsuit, MoPop brings these sacred bits of our shared culture to the masses year-round.

325 Fifth Ave. N., 206-770-2700
mopop.org

HIT THE ART SPOTS
ON FIRST THURSDAYS

While there are several regular art walk options in the city, from Ballard to Capitol Hill, the premier route to take begins in Pioneer Square every first Thursday of the month. Pioneer Square, one of the city's oldest and most historic districts, is home to gallery after gallery of eye-catching work. And curious art lovers will find ample wine and spirits along the way to spark moments of inspiration. Don't be surprised if you're surrounded by many other fans as you admire work from Seattle creators or those from around the state. While some say that Pioneer Square is haunted by the ghosts of a Seattle long gone, that's no reason not to get out of the house and walk among the spirits, feeling spirited and drinking spirits while getting your art on.

Pioneer Square, 206-667-0687
pioneersquare.org/experiences/first-thursday-art-walk

TIP
If you're a drinker, bring a flask. Why not? YOLO!

WATCH FILMS
FROM ALL OVER THE WORLD

Get your popcorn! It's movie time! Every spring, Seattle International Film Festival takes over Seattle for an epic cascade of movie magic. For about four weeks, the SIFF shows hundreds of movies from nearly one hundred countries to a wide audience. Annual attendance tops 150,000 people, making SIFF the largest film festival in the United States and one of the largest in the world. Showing everything from documentaries to animated shorts, the festival has wowed audiences for nearly five decades. Each year, celebrities of the silver screen visit Seattle to talk about their projects or expound upon an acting experience. During the rest of the year, SIFF maintains a strong presence in Seattle, operating several important movie houses, including the SIFF Cinema Uptown, which shows the latest hits as well as art house gems.

Seattle International Film Festival (SIFF)
206-464-5830 (general), 206-324-9996 (showtimes & tickets)
siff.net

SIFF Cinema Uptown
511 Queen Anne Ave. N., 206-464-5830
siff.net/year-round-cinema/cinema-venues/siff-cinema-uptown

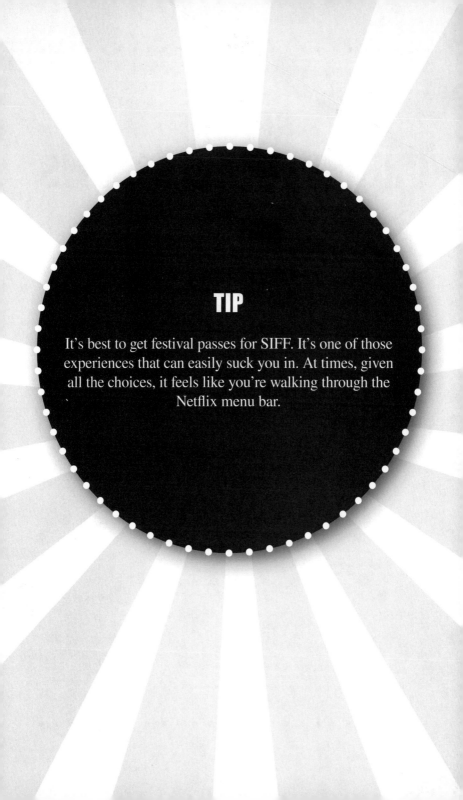

TIP

It's best to get festival passes for SIFF. It's one of those experiences that can easily suck you in. At times, given all the choices, it feels like you're walking through the Netflix menu bar.

SEE THE
CHERRY TREE BLOSSOMS
AT UW

For a few beautiful weeks each spring, the cherry blossoms outside Gerberding Hall on the campus of the University of Washington exceed everything else in the city in beauty. The scene is so picturesque that it attracts tourists from overseas to come and take pictures amidst the beautiful boughs. Some lie beneath the trees, hoping a silk-like petal or two from the blooms will fall and caress their faces. Others climb to pose among the curling branches as if to say, this is one form of paradise. On the one hand, it's sad that the beauty only lasts a few weeks, often in the midst of March, if the city is lucky. On the other, the fleeting nature of the whole experience adds to the urgency of bearing witness to this local wonder.

Gerberding Hall, 206-543-9198
washington.edu/visit/

SEE TODAY'S GREAT WORKS
AT THE FRYE

Opened in 1952, the Frye Art Museum, located in the Emerald City's First Hill neighborhood, is free and open to the public for visits. The museum, which focuses on contemporary art and artists, began in the mid-twentieth century after a donation by Charles and Emma Frye and shares a vision with its founders for public service and artistic curiosity. Past exhibitions have included photographs from Manuel Álvarez Bravo, also known as Mexico's poet of light; marionettes dressed in pastel suits; and Ko Kirk Yamahira's deconstructed paintings. And while the layout of the beautiful exhibits at the Frye is always clean, crisp, and polished, the art itself will provoke and astonish and make you remember that not all great works come from hundreds or thousands of years ago; some great works are being made and shown today.

704 Terry Ave., 206-622-9250
fryemuseum.org

EXPERIENCE AMERICA'S ROOTS
AT NAAM

It's a long-held aphorism of artists: it's easy to destroy but difficult to create. And, in the case of the Northwest African American Museum, this remains true. What began as an idea in 1983 finally became reality in 2008, some twenty-five years after its conception. Nevertheless—and thankfully—the museum exists today. It's home to African history, art, and displays of culture from people who came to America as slaves and also as immigrants from countries like Somalia, Sudan, and Ethiopia. Past exhibitions have included photos by artists Jessica Rycheal and Zorn B. Taylor on the intersections and identities that are held within blackness, a tribute to the dancers and dance theater of Harlem in the early twentieth century, and a commemoration of positive black characters on Saturday morning cartoons from the 1970s.

2300 S. Massachusetts St., 206-518-6000
naamnw.org

VISIT
THE REFURBISHED AAM

Another branch of the Seattle Art Museum, the Asian Art Museum, has historically been a center for celebrating the art and culture of Asia, as well as the heritage of many Seattleites. Along with the display of many beautifully crafted and historic artifacts at the museum are the facility's popular Arts in Action series, lectures, films, and visual arts events. The AAM is currently undergoing a $54 million renovation and expansion of its historic art deco building. The museum is expected to reopen in 2019; in the meantime, see some of the collection highlights at the Seattle Art Museum—which will just increase your appetite for the grand reopening!

1400 E. Prospect St., 206-654-3210
seattleartmuseum.org/visit/asian-art-museum

SURROUND YOURSELF
WITH THE INDUSTRY
OF THE NORTHWEST

Lake Union is one of the most picturesque areas in Seattle. And sitting right on the edge of the water is the Museum of History & Industry, a monument to some of the most inspiring innovations and stories in the Northwest's illustrious history. The museum, striking building and all, was established in Seattle because of the region's connection to industry of all kinds—from Amazon to Boeing to Microsoft—amidst some of the most extraordinary natural beauty in the country. Past exhibits have included the actual flag carried to Omaha Beach on D-Day, a retrospective on how people cook and eat in the Northwest, and a history of Seattle film and movie theaters. MOHAI, as the place is affectionately called, is a terrific blend of excitement and history, which makes for a great afternoon.

860 Terry Ave. N., 206-324-1126
mohai.org

TAKE
THE STAIRS

Something many who live in the city don't know is that Seattle is an extremely widespread metropolis. You can start in the far reaches of Ballard and walk to the Heaven Sent Fried Chicken in Renton. It would take you around six hours to do it, but you'd be safe to undertake the mission—and ready for some delicious bird when you were done. And a major reason the city, which is built on hills, is so friendly to walkers is the web of charming staircases—some short, some that go up forever—scattered throughout Seattle. They're so abundant that walking up and down them—the world's original StairMaster!—is the preferred way to exercise for many residents. There is even a three-hundred-page book, which we recommend, dedicated to the entire network of stairs: *Seattle Stairway Walks: An Up-and-Down Guide to City Neighborhoods,* by Cathy and Jake Jaramillo. When you're done with this tome in your hand, check that one out.

seattlestairwaywalks.com

SPREAD YOUR WINGS
AT THE MUSEUM OF FLIGHT

It's true that much of Seattle's modern history includes digital giants like Microsoft and Amazon. And that trend doesn't seem to be stopping soon (Hello, new Facebook offices!). But the Emerald City also has a long relationship with more tactile industries—most notably, Boeing and air travel. "So," people thought, "let's make a museum!" And they did. The Museum of Flight is full of history, but even more full of planes—from models to actual aircraft. You can sit inside some of them or watch how air travel is used to explore the sky and stars. If humanity has proven one thing, it's that we always want to push the boundaries and see what's beyond the ridge. See how we've done it around the world at the Museum of Flight.

9404 E. Marginal Way S., 206-764-5700
museumofflight.org

OTHER PLACES TO TRY

Seattle has so much to offer in the way of the arts, from the very finest of fine art to the simplest DIY. For the budding artist in you, get lessons and art supplies at Dancing Brush Studio in Ballard.

Dancing Brush Studio
5129 Ballard Ave. NW, 206-782-2882
dancingbrushstudio.com

ENLIVEN MINDS
AT A MUSEUM MADE FOR KIDS

It can be nearly impossible to get kids to go to the museum. Either they refuse outright or, upon walking through the doors, they decide they need sleep, food, or to throw a tantrum. But that's why the Seattle Children's Museum was created: to give kids the enjoyment of discovery without adding the heft of history and self-importance to the equation. Inside, the museum is interactive. Kids can climb tree forts, pretend to fish, kick a soccer ball, or learn to grocery shop. And, if they get hungry, there's a cafeteria on-site to satisfy those pizza cravings. The museum, which is designed for children ten months to ten years, offers myriad exploratory exhibits in its many spaces—from COG city to the Imagination Studio to the Global Village.

305 Harrison St., 206-441-1768
thechildrensmuseum.org

SNAP A PHOTO
WITH THE FREMONT TROLL

With a big, bulbous nose and large, reaching hands, the *Fremont Troll* seems to emerge out of the rock from which it was carved. You can visit the outstanding structure at just about any point in the day, and you'll see admirers taking photos, painting it on canvas, or just posing on the structure. The public art piece, commissioned by the Fremont Arts Council and created by a handful of artists in 1990, was inspired by Scandinavian folklore and is a nod to that region's rich history in the Emerald City. The work was meant to beautify a small part of the city that had previously been populated by drug addicts. The troll, which is eighteen feet tall and weighs about thirteen thousand pounds, is made of concrete and is buttressed by wire and steel rebar to make it look looming and lifelike.

Troll Ave. N. (under the Aurora Bridge at N. Thirty-Sixth St.)
fremont.com/explore/sights/troll/

BLOW A BUBBLE
AND PUT IT ON THE GUM WALL

Post Alley, underneath historic Pike Place Market, is one of the most storied little passages in the entire Emerald City. There are restaurants and shops there that have existed for decades and decades, along with the beloved Unexpected Productions improv theater nearby. But perhaps the most notable aspect of that particular area is the famed gum wall. There, thousands of chewers who have come before you have chewed up their sticks of gum and stuck them to the generations-old brick walls. Red, yellow, green, blue, white, and neon gum polka-dot the walls, some stretched in long rubbery strands, some still in bubble form. It's a community art piece that provides a weird fruit-flavored smell for each ocean breeze that comes through and that tourists in the city can't help but put in selfies.

Gum Wall
1428 Post Alley

Unexpected Productions
1428 Post Alley, 206-587-2414
unexpectedproductions.org

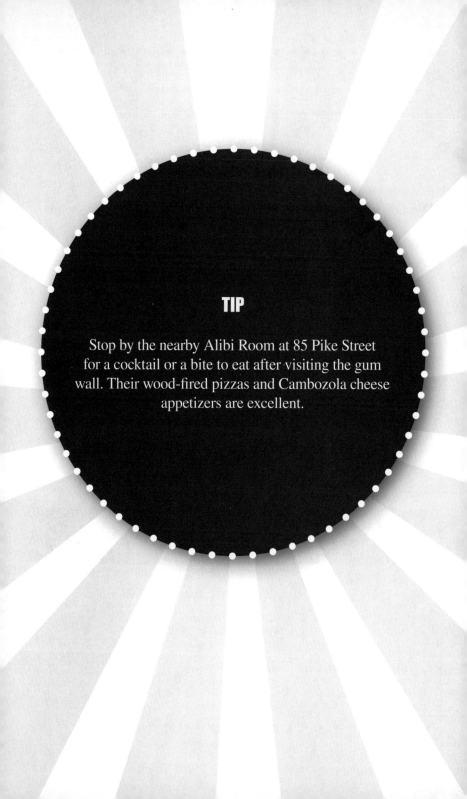

TIP

Stop by the nearby Alibi Room at 85 Pike Street for a cocktail or a bite to eat after visiting the gum wall. Their wood-fired pizzas and Cambozola cheese appetizers are excellent.

VISIT
BRUCE LEE'S GRAVE

Whenever people think of the greatest martial artist, the conversation ultimately lands on Bruce Lee. It's like when people bring up the best guitarists of all time—Jimi Hendrix is the final answer. But, as with Hendrix, not everyone who loves him knows that he's from Seattle. Lee was such an integral part of Seattle that his grave remains here. The landmark headstone can be found at Lake View Cemetery, which welcomes visitors to come and pay their respects to the man who made himself famous for precise kicks, swift punches, and enduring a claw to his svelte chest. Honored right next to the pioneer is the gravestone for Lee's son, Brandon. Adorned with gold lettering, the father and son lie in peace side by side for the world to honor.

1554 Fifteenth Ave. E., 206-322-1582
lakeviewcemeteryassociation.com

TIP
Be respectful. Remember, you're in a graveyard.

IMPRESS YOUR DATE
AT TEATRO ZINZANNI

Seattle is one of the most creative cities in the country and as a result, there are many great places to have a meal and see a fantastic show. You can't go wrong with the classy Triple Door or the surreal Café Nordo, but we recommend, above all else, Teatro ZinZanni, the most epic of them all. Nowhere else can you see a man juggle glowing balls of light while a woman swings from a trapeze one hundred feet off the ground, a world-class band plays impossibly difficult pieces, and the wait staff serves you a cocktail while a magician pulls a rabbit from a hat. If it sounds like a lot, it is. In the best of ways. It's wonderful magic, a delicious meal, and more than a few memories.

The Triple Door
216 Union St., 206-838-4333
thetripledoor.net

Café Nordo
109 S. Main St.
cafenordo.com

Teatro ZinZanni
6046 West Lake Sammamish Pkwy. NE, Redmond, 206-802-0015
zinzanni.com/seattle

GET THE CELEB VIBE
ON LOCAL MOVIE SETS

The Emerald City is famous for two movies more than any others, both '90s classics. Synonymous with the city are 1992's *Singles* and 1993's *Sleepless in Seattle.* If you were to walk by it, you might just miss it, but nestled in a little area of east Capitol Hill, just above the bustling Fifteenth Avenue East, are a few row houses called the Coryell Court Apartments that were made famous by *Singles,* a story about grungy young adults trying to figure out their lives while listening to alt-rock. Or you can visit the waterfront and check out the location of Tom Hanks's houseboat in *Sleepless,* a story about finding love through the radio. Still bobbing on the banks of Lake Union off Westlake Avenue N., the cute white cabin-like structure is there for the whole world to see.

OTHER PLACES TO VISIT

There's tons to see in Seattle. Pretty much anywhere you go, there's something odd and wonderful happening. Check out the performances at The Pink Door, Julia's On Broadway, or Can Can if you like vaudeville acts.

The Pink Door
1919 Post Alley, 206-443-3241
thepinkdoor.net

Julia's on Broadway
300 Broadway E., 206-860-1818
lefauxshow.com

Can Can
94 Pike St., 206-652-0832
thecancan.com

TURN THE PAGE
AT FANTAGRAPHICS

Nestled in the unassuming, industrial Georgetown neighborhood, Fantagraphics Books & Gallery is home to some of the most important comic books in America today. Many things get their unfair share of praise these days, but the happiness that Fantagraphics elicits is real. "Fantagraphics has published and championed many of the finest cartoonists working today," says the *New York Times.* In the Georgetown shop, readers can check out everything the publisher has in print as well as comics from other publishers. The space, which hosts readings and screenings, is home to a rotating exhibit each month. And while Fantagraphics doesn't put out the likes of, say, the *X-Men* or *Spider-Man,* it is responsible for many favorites in the comics world.

1201 S. Vale St., 1-800-657-1100
fantagraphics.com

TIP
Fantagraphics is one of the weirdest and most "out there" book publishers in the country. Be prepared for anything when you walk through its hallowed doors.

SHOPPING AND FASHION

DISCOVER YOUR STYLE
AT TRAILER PARK MALL

Inside one of the eight nostalgic silver trailers, you might find an old deer skull perfect for your mantelpiece. Or you might happen upon the just-right fluffy boa to wear with the form-fitting black dress you bought for twelve dollars from one of the other trailers in this interconnected horseshoe arrangement. Indeed, at the Georgetown Trailer Park Mall, you're amidst a fun and kitschy Venn diagram of thrift shop, vintage toy store, and your great grandparents' junk drawers, where you can sift through rare clothing, jewelry, costumes, motorcycle gearhead paraphernalia, and home furnishings curated by artists and quirky shopkeepers. It's the perfect place to stop before heading off to one of the cute Georgetown neighborhood cafés or bars in this up-and-coming South End district.

5805 Airport Way S.
georgetowntrailerpark.com

GLAMORIZE
AT THE PRETTY PARLOR

It's a rare occasion that the city of Seattle finds itself on any glamour magazine's top ten list of the best dressed. But that certainly doesn't mean that the area is devoid of fashion. In fact, between all the folks wearing black jeans, flannel shirts, and sweatshirts, there are many prominent beauties—from rock 'n' roll front women to drag queens to burlesque and boylesque performers—and nearly every single one of these lovely folks shops at the Pretty Parlor. From elaborate and elegant pink evening dresses to strings of pearls to makeup kits complete with a My Little Pony earring holder, the Capitol Hill neighborhood shop is a pink Pandora's box of all that's glittery and glitzy for the star in your life.

119 Summit Ave. E., 206-405-CUTE (2883)
prettyparlor.com

POPPIN' TAGS
AT A GINORMOUS GOODWILL

When you park your car and walk through the front doors of the Seattle Goodwill, one of the biggest vintage stores in the United States, you have something on your mind that you need to purchase—whether it's a new set of pots and pans, a flannel shirt, a pair of work boots, or a Ninja Turtle coffee mug. But when you leave the store, you're likely carrying a couple of vinyl records, a set of cooking knives, and a Seattle Seahawks hoodie. In other words, the Seattle Goodwill is sprawling and filled to the brim with the sort of fun items—like moccasins, velour jumpsuits, luggage, and even zebra jammies—that the Emerald City rapper Macklemore made famous in his platinum-selling ode to discount shopping, "Thrift Shop."

1400 S. Lane St., 206-860-5711
seattlegoodwill.org/locations/30

TIP
Really give yourself some time when you stop by. There is always more than meets the eye in a Goodwill. And the Lane Street location is as vast as they come.

LOSE YOURSELF
IN THE FREMONT VINTAGE MALL

While there are other more conventional shopping malls in the city—from Northgate to Westlake to Pacific Place—the Fremont Vintage Mall is much worthier of your time. In Seattle, as prices continue to rise for rent and retail, many of the vintage stores remain affordable. And here, the world is your oyster. Explore thousands of square feet of classic clothing, toys, furniture, books, records, and dinnerware among people who have an eye for style in this one-stop spot for vintage, antiques, and thrift and consignment goods. Take home a rabbit fur Russian hat when you thought you were going in for a set of teacups in this community-based market.

3419 Fremont Pl. N., 206-329-4460
fremontvintagemall.com

EQUIP YOURSELF
WITH CLASSIC KICKS DOWNTOWN

Putting foot to pavement in downtown Seattle, you'll likely see any number of clothing shops to frequent, from the chic to the more understated classic contemporary. But the place you'll have the most fun—the one where, upon making your purchase, you will feel both stylish and exuberant—is Sneaker City. In the cool shadow of Pike Place Market, Sneaker City shines its boutique light on the retro-loving sneakerhead in all of us. From bright red Nikes with black swooshes to Seattle Mariner-colored kicks to classic Jordans, the longtime authority on sneakers remains one of the hotspots in Seattle—and is perfect for the kid in all of us who still holds onto the hope that one more inflated air bubble in the heel of a shoe will make for flight.

110 Pike St., 206-621-7923
facebook.com/seattlesneakercity

OTHER PLACES TO TRY

Jax Joon for cute accessories and knickknacks, Trove for lovely vintage clothing, and the University Village shopping mall for an assortment of clothes, tech gadgets, books, and food.

Jax Joon
5338 Ballard Ave., 206-789-8777
jaxjoon.com

Trove Vintage Boutique and Bridal
2204 NW Market St., 206-297-6068
trovevintage.blogspot.com

University Village
2623 NE University Village St., 206-523-0622
uvillage.com

ACTIVITIES
BY SEASON

SPRING

SUMMER

FALL

WINTER

SUGGESTED
ITINERARIES

OUTDOOR ACTIVITIES

FAMILY TIME

THE FANTASTICAL

CELEBRITY-FOCUSED

BEST FOOD & DRINK DAY

INDEX